DAY AND NIGHT IN THE Rainforest

by Ellen Labrecque

raintree
a Capstone company — publishers for children

Raintree is an imprint of Capstone Global Library Limited, a company incorporated in England and Wales having its registered office at 264 Banbury Road, Oxford, OX2 7DY – Registered company number: 6695582

www.raintree.co.uk
myorders@raintree.co.uk

Edited by Jessica Rusick
Designed by Hilary Wacholz
Original illustrations © Capstone Global Library Limited 2023
Picture research by Kelly Doudna
Originated by Capstone Global Library Ltd
Printed and bound in India

978 1 3982 4184 8 (hardback)
978 1 3982 4185 5 (paperback)

British Library Cataloguing in Publication Data
A full catalogue record for this book is available from the British Library.

Acknowledgements
We would like to thank the following for permission to reproduce photographs: iStockphoto: MmeEmil, Cover (scarlet macaw), 1, slowmotiongli, 17; Mighty Media, Inc.: 20, 21; Shutterstock: buteo, 18, DanielSnake, 13, Dennis Stogsdill, 7, Dirk Ercken, 14, Fotos593, 5, Jamen Percy, 15, Kevin Wells Photography, 11, kingma photos, 9, Leonardo Mercon, 16, MarcusVDT, 8, Ondrej Prosicky, 19, Photo Spirit, 6, pyzata, Cover (rain forest), 1, Ryan M. Bolton, 10

Every effort has been made to contact copyright holders of material reproduced in this book. Any omissions will be rectified in subsequent printings if notice is given to the publisher.

All the internet addresses (URLs) given in this book were valid at the time of going to press. However, due to the dynamic nature of the internet, some addresses may have changed, or sites may have changed or ceased to exist since publication. While the author and publisher regret any inconvenience this may cause readers, no responsibility for any such changes can be accepted by either the author or the publisher.

Contents

Words in **bold** are in the glossary.

What is a rainforest?

Rainforests are wet forest **habitats**. They have many tall trees. There are rainforests around the world. Some are in Central and South America.

Many animals live in rainforests. Some come out during the day. Others come out at night.

Find out more

Books

Rainforest (Fact Cat: Habitats), Izzi Howell (Wayland, 2015)

Rainforests (Animal Homes), John Wood
(Booklife Publishing, 2017)

Tropical Rainforests (Amazing Habitats), Leon Gray
(Franklin Watts, 2014)

Websites

www.bbc.co.uk/bitesize/topics/zx882hv
Learn more about habitats and the environment.

**www.dkfindout.com/uk/animals-and-nature/habitats-
and-ecosystems**
Find out more about animal habitats around the world.

Index

About the author

Ellen Labrecque is the author of more than 100 non-fiction children's books. She lives in Pennsylvania, USA, with her husband and two kids. She has the best writing partner in the world – her dog, Oscar. An avid reader and runner, Ellen is a morning person. On most days, she is up before the sun.